S0-AQM-415

TALES FROM THE CRISPER

TALES FROM THE CRISPER

A Spirited Fruit & Vegetable Guide to Life

From the creators of

METRO BOOKS
NEW YORK

2006 Metro Books

ISBN-13: 978-0-7607-8110-4
ISBN-10: 0-7607-8110-9

Printed and bound in Singapore by KHL

1   3   5   7   9   10   8   6   4   2

....

Endpapers: © Richard Hutchings/Corbis

CHAPTER OPENER PHOTOGRAPHY CREDITS
Chapter 1: Sunflowers: Photodisc/Punchstock; Sign: © Paul A. Souders/Corbis
Chapter 2: © Walter Hodges/The Image Bank/Getty Images
Chapter 3: Photodisc/Punchstock
Chapter 4: © Photolibrary.com/Photonica/Getty Images
Chapter 5: © Kim Blaxland/Stone/Getty Images
Chapter 6: © Malcom Fife/zefa/Corbis
Chapter 7: © Megan Maloy/Photonica/Getty Images

CONTENTS

INTRODUCTION

AS COUNTLESS POETS AND WRITERS, songwriters, painters, and self-help gurus have recognized, the challenges of day-to-day living are fairly universal, however much we'd like to think that we (and, by extension, our problems) are unique. Who among us hasn't wrestled with a difficult familial relationship or tussled with a coworker? How many of us haven't struggled at some point in our lives to exercise more and eat less? And is there anyone who can honestly claim they've never thrown their hands up in frustration because a new technological innovation has presented an insurmountable challenge to the Luddite buried deep inside?

Take a deep breath and consider this: misery loves company, so you should take comfort in the fact that generations of people just like you have suffered in much the same way. Yes, life can be overwhelming, but there are many ways to deal with its trials and tribulations. Whether the answer is psychotherapy, tantric yoga, or drinking decaffeinated coffee, many strategies for coping with the vicissitudes of daily existence have evolved over the centuries. The very fact that you hold this book in your hands shows that you are ready to accept that there are probably solutions out there to your problems, and moreover, that you could do worse than taking the time to learn from the experiences of others.

Ask yourself: "What are the least stressed-out organisms on the planet?" For obvious reasons, humans are out of the running (just look at yourself in the mirror sometime!), and so are most other members of the animal kingdom, too, thanks to the increasing encroachments of civilization on Earth's natural habitats. No, for an example of a truly relaxed approach to living, we must turn to the domesticated fruits and vegetables we welcome to our tables every day. Lovingly planted in rich, loamy soil, carefully protected against drought and savage attacks by ravenous insects, and gently coaxed to the full potential of their maturity, producekind is ideally groomed to be the most laid-back life form around.

Having studied carefully at the roots of our serene, vitamin-rich friends, we have compiled a book full of useful advice and cautionary examples to aid you as you strive to achieve your own inner calm. If you need help in matters of the heart, or with a troublesome situation at work; if you are contemplating a trip but are nervous about your preparations; or if you'd like to acquire some new hobbies to fill your free time more constructively, consider the suggestions of your seeded, pulpy pals. At the very least, they can tell you how to eat more healthily: eat more meat, and give all those fun-loving fruits and vegetables a break!

CHAPTER 1
PLANTING YOUR SEED

THE INS AND OUTS OF BEAUTY DATING AND LOVE

Everyone knows that a truly fulfilling life requires a modicum of meaningful companionship. But whether you're looking for love, in need of a quickie, or tired of playing solitaire, finding a partner is frequently a lot harder than you might think. Of course, the pursuit of a soul mate raises a host of related issues: if you're currently "on the market," just how important is it to keep up appearances? What do you do if your partner is cheating on you? And how does one cope with the (occasionally) disagreeable habits of our husbands and wives? For answers to these and many others of love's mysteries, we turn to producekind for guidance.

MAINTAINING
A HEALTHY
SEX LIFE
MEANS ALWAYS
BEING OPEN
TO NEW
EXPERIENCES

Mademoiselle Dominatrix drove her subjects plum crazy with desire.

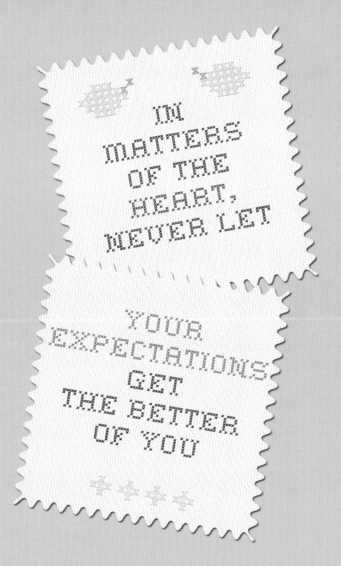

IN MATTERS OF THE HEART, NEVER LET

YOUR EXPECTATIONS GET THE BETTER OF YOU

IN LOVE,
AS IN WORK,
IT IS
ESSENTIAL
TO LOOK
YOUR BEST

NEVER
FORGET
THE
LASTING
NATURE
OF FIRST
IMPRESSIONS

MENU

Roast chicken without vegetables £4.50
8oz rump steak (no vegetables) £6.95
Red Thai curry and rice £5.50
Jacket potatoes £2.95 OFF
Sandwiches (meat only) £2.95
Paté and toast £2.50

Ice cream and chocolate sauce £1.95
Spotted dick and custard £2.50

Coffee and mints £1.00

Initially, the pear found the passion fruit a little overbearing.

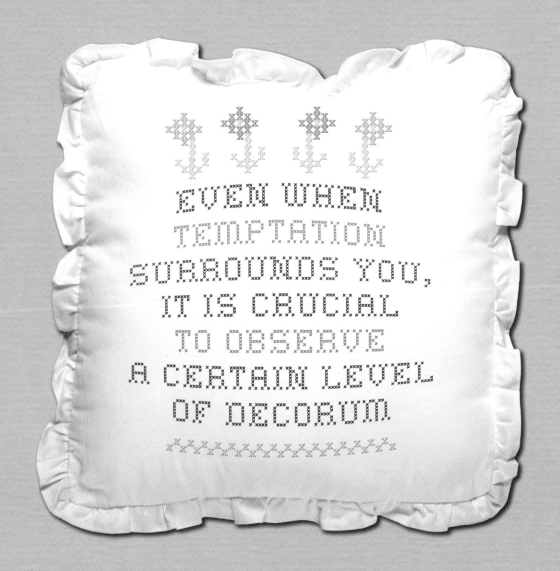

EVEN WHEN TEMPTATION SURROUNDS YOU, IT IS CRUCIAL TO OBSERVE A CERTAIN LEVEL OF DECORUM

Mr. Braeburn gave the au pear
a big goose for Christmas.

KEEPING
SECRETS CAN
BE FATAL
IN A
RELATIONSHIP

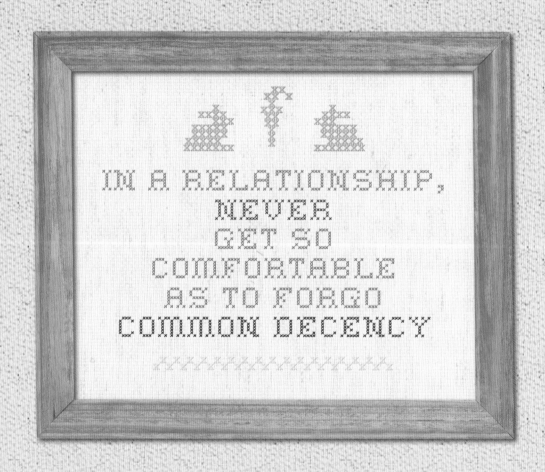

IN A RELATIONSHIP,
NEVER
GET SO
COMFORTABLE
AS TO FORGO
COMMON DECENCY

Edwina once again found her sleep
interrupted by Eddie's digestive irregularities.

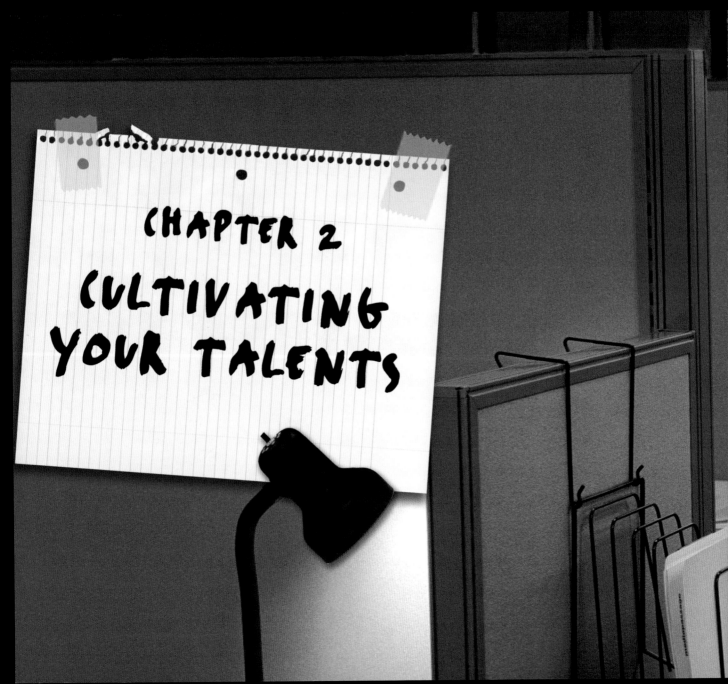

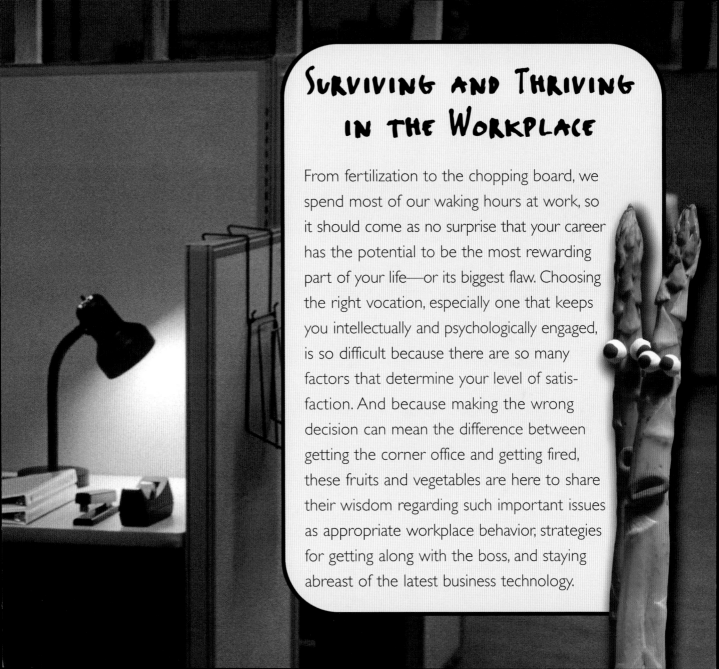

Surviving and Thriving in the Workplace

From fertilization to the chopping board, we spend most of our waking hours at work, so it should come as no surprise that your career has the potential to be the most rewarding part of your life—or its biggest flaw. Choosing the right vocation, especially one that keeps you intellectually and psychologically engaged, is so difficult because there are so many factors that determine your level of satisfaction. And because making the wrong decision can mean the difference between getting the corner office and getting fired, these fruits and vegetables are here to share their wisdom regarding such important issues as appropriate workplace behavior, strategies for getting along with the boss, and staying abreast of the latest business technology.

31

AT CERTAIN
TIMES IN
YOUR CAREER,
YOU MAY HAVE
TO BE A LITTLE
AGGRESSIVE

DON'T
LET
MANAGEMENT
STIFLE
YOUR
INDIVIDUALITY

HARD WORK
PAYS
OFF
IN THE END

The best thing about Eddie's new job was the huge celery.

IT'S IMPORTANT
TO STAND UP
FOR
YOURSELF
IN THE
WORKPLACE

Hazel resigned because she was tired of working for peanuts.

IN THE INFORMATION AGE, THE MOST SUCCESSFUL

BUSINESSES KEEP ABREAST OF CUTTING-EDGE TECHNOLOGY

The pears made many fruitless attempts to send and receive e-mails on their new Blackberries.

ALWAYS REMEMBER TO BEHAVE PROFESSIONALLY AT THE OFFICE

Kevin had spent the entire day downloading corn on the Internet.

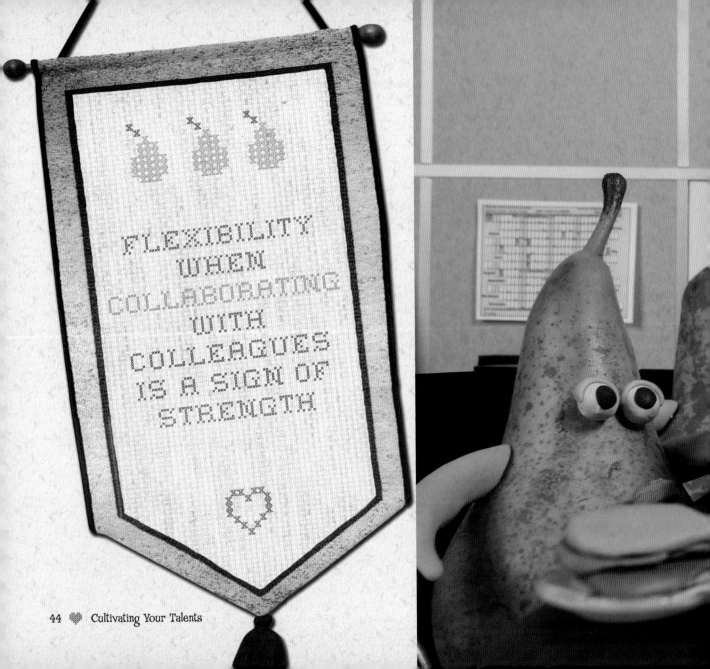

FLEXIBILITY
WHEN
COLLABORATING
WITH
COLLEAGUES
IS A SIGN OF
STRENGTH

The pears tried to arrange a follow-up meeting, but unfortunately the dates kept clashing.

CELEBRATE YOUR SUCCESSES

When the awards were announced, the winners went totally bananas.

DON'T GET TOO DRUNK AT OFFICE FUNCTIONS, IT COULD COME BACK TO HAUNT YOU IN THE END

Relaxing at Home
and
Pursuing Your Hobbies

After all your hard work putting food on the table and keeping a roof over your head, you deserve a break. And because your free time is precious, you need to make the most of it. Of course, everyone has their own interpretation of relaxation: for some it means watching television or listening to music, for others it means taking up a hobby or two, and to many it means simply spending quality time with the family. Whatever your fancy, you need to maximize your leisure time, take advantage of the holidays, and have fun! And if you need some fresh ideas about how to make the most of your non-working hours, your juicy, vitamin-laden comrades are happy to provide some expert advice.

TO
BE A
WELL-
ROUNDED
INDIVIDUAL,
IT'S

IMPORTANT
TO HAVE
A WIDE
RANGE
OF
INTERESTS

p

WHEN
SHARING
WITH
OTHERS,
DON'T
BE AFRAID
TO REVEAL
YOUR SOFTER
SIDE

REMEMBER
THAT, FOR SOME,
THE HOLIDAYS
CAN BE A
PARTICULARLY
PAINFUL TIME
OF YEAR

IF YOU HAVE ANY BIZARRE HABITS, IT'S BEST TO PRACTICE THEM IN THE PRIVACY OF YOUR OWN HOME

KEEPING UP WITH TRENDS CAN BE A CRUCIAL PART OF A TEENAGER'S SOCIAL LIFE

EVEN AT HOME, FLATTERY

CAN OFTEN GET YOU WHAT YOU WANT

The baby corns tried to butter up their mother.

MAKE
THE MOST
OF YOUR
LEISURE
TIME —
YOU'VE
EARNED IT

TRADITION IS THE KEY TO CELEBRATING THE HOLIDAY SEASON WITH FRIENDS AND FAMILY

On the first day of Christmas my true love sent to me, a parsnip in a pear tree.

69

CHAPTER 4
PEST CONTROL

Health Risks and Other Hazards of Modern Life

Unfortunately, life isn't all fun and games. The world is a dangerous place and you need to constantly be on your toes. Among the many challenges that daily remind us of the fleeting nature of our lives are diseases, man-made catastrophes, and natural disasters. Because of the dangers that lurk, the inhabitants of your produce drawer encourage you to be aware of your surroundings at all times. You may think you are invincible, but even the mighty can succumb to violent waters, a vehicular mishap, or the perils of alcohol. By encouraging you to stay vigilant and to learn from the mistakes of others, these members of the plant kingdom hope to help you avoid doing any damage to yourself, your loved ones, or your property.

The walnut wasn't sure whether it was just a splitting headache or something a little more serious...

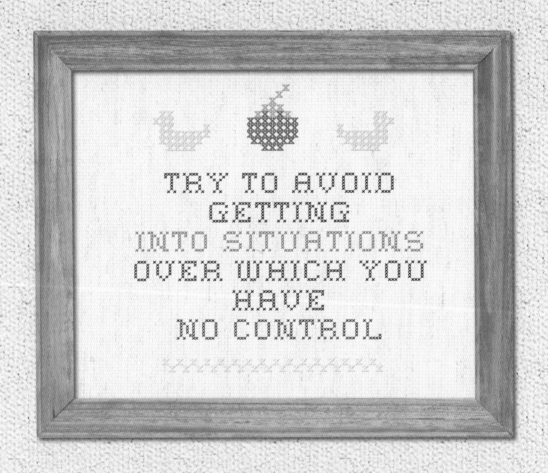

TRY TO AVOID GETTING INTO SITUATIONS OVER WHICH YOU HAVE NO CONTROL

Tom swam for his life, but the currants were too strong for him.

IN
THE
MODERN
AGE,
IT'S
ESSENTIAL

TO
HAVE
ADEQUATE
HEALTH
COVERAGE

WHEN
NATURE
CALLS,
YOU MUST
ANSWER.

After a liquid fertilizer lunch, the pumpkin was desperate for a leek.

ALWAYS
LOOK BOTH WAYS
BEFORE
CROSSING
THE STREET

WHILE
IT'S GOOD
TO BE HANDY,
DON'T
BE AFRAID
TO CALL A
PROFESSIONAL

The plumber was called in when they found a really bad leek in the bathroom.

AGING
CAN BE A
PAINFUL PROCESS,
BUT IT
HAPPENS
TO EVERYONE

WHEN
DANGER
LOOMS,

DON'T
GO
DOWN
WITHOUT
A FIGHT

The sage and onions were looking at a fate worse than a fate worse than death.

EXCESSIVE
DRINKING
CAN
BE
LETHAL

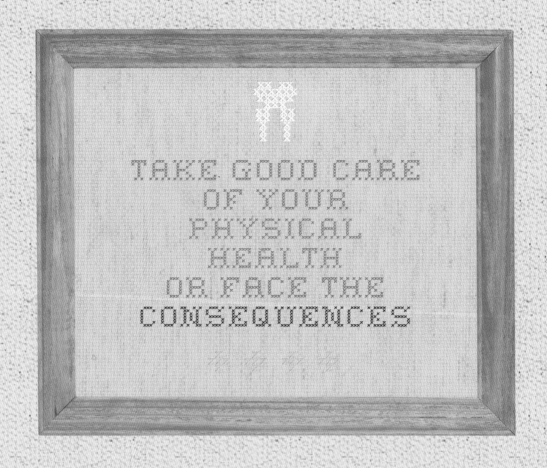

Eddie went to the dentist
and had to have three fillings.

Expanding Your Horizons Through the Wonder of Travel

It's time to get out and see the world! Travel can provide unparalleled rewards, ranging from relaxation to adventure to an increased understanding of the universe around us. Because of these benefits, and many others besides, everyone should experience the joy of exploring distant locales; in fact, it is essential to becoming a well-rounded individual. However, traveling requires quite a bit of preparation and there are some essential things to be aware of before setting out on a trip. Your pulpy, fibrous friends are ready to address your many concerns about planning a trip, from travel agents to airport security to observing other countries' customs.

WHEN FLYING, MAKE SURE

YOU'RE AWARE OF ALL THE AIRPORT SECURITY RULES

GIVE
THE GIFT
OF
TRAVEL

IT'S
IMPORTANT
TO DO
YOUR
RESEARCH
BEFORE
GOING
ON A
BIG TRIP

WHEN PLANNING A TRIP,

MAKE SURE TO USE A REPUTABLE TRAVEL AGENT

BE
WELCOMING
TO
ALL
NEWCOMERS

On arrival, the migrants were overwhelmed to be greeted in person by the star-spangled banana.

DON'T BE AFRAID TO EXPLORE THE FAR REACHES OF THE UNIVERSE

It was one small step for man, one giant leek for mankind.

NEVER PERSECUTE ANOTHER BECAUSE OF SUPERFICIAL DIFFERENCES

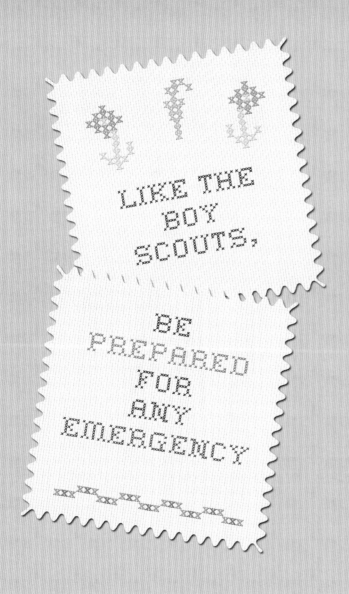

LIKE THE
BOY
SCOUTS,

BE
PREPARED
FOR
ANY
EMERGENCY

The survivors had been adrift for so long that even the lime had scurvy.

CHAPTER 6

BEWARE ROTTEN PRODUCE

AVOIDING VIOLENT VEGGIES AND OTHER DISREPUTABLE CHARACTERS

Unfortunately, not everyone is made of sugar and spice and everything nice. There are a lot of bad characters out there, and it is crucial to protect yourself from their machinations as best you can. The first step is to know your vulnerabilities and, armed with that knowledge, take steps to protect yourself from the attempts of others to exploit them. Of course, if you ever do find yourself in the wrong place at the wrong time, you need to know how to defend yourself from a terrible bruising—or worse. A few simple pointers from these fruits and veggies, including some cautionary examples, are guaranteed to go far in preventing you from such evils as mugging, being conned, and Peeping Toms.

SOMETIMES
JUSTICE

IS MORE
THAN
JUST
BLIND

6'6"

6'0"

5'6"

DON'T
PLAY
WITH
YOUR FOOD

THE GRASS
MAY NOT ALWAYS
BE GREENER
ON THE
OTHER SIDE

Once in the city, the coconuts suddenly realized that maybe paradise wasn't so bad after all.

THANK YOUR LUCKY STARS THE POLICE ARE ON THE JOB

There was no doubt about it, they were now looking for a cereal killer.

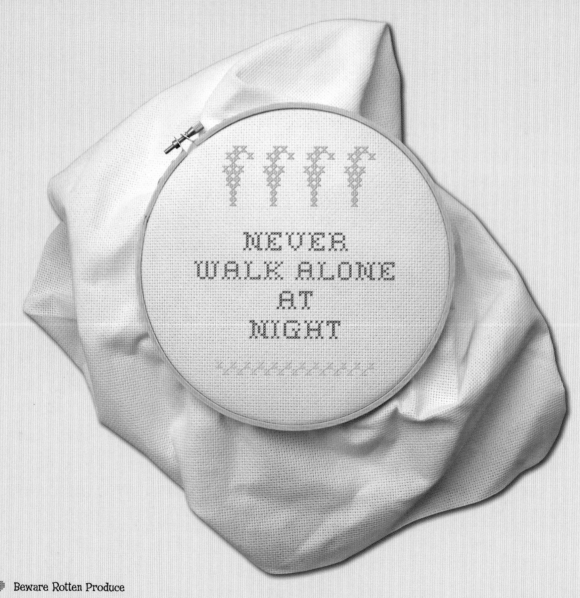

NEVER
WALK ALONE
AT
NIGHT

The carrots had a pea
up against the wall.

ALWAYS
CLOSE

YOUR
CURTAINS

Mary didn't scrub
up too badly for
an old potato.

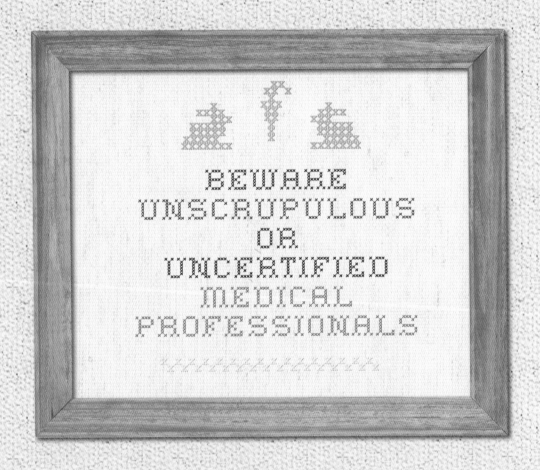

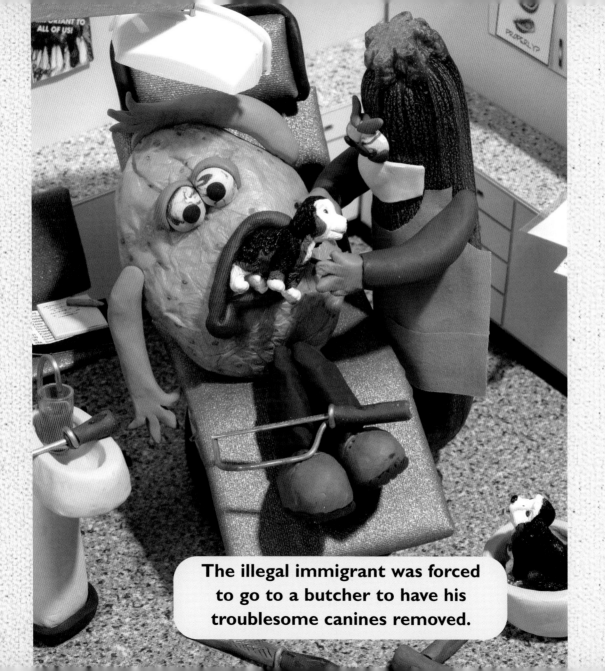

The illegal immigrant was forced to go to a butcher to have his troublesome canines removed.

BE
CAREFUL
WHAT
YOU
WISH FOR

BUYER
BEWARE,
ESPECIALLY
WHEN IT
COMES
TO
USED
GOODS

Chapter 7
EAT MEAT!

Improving Your Diet
and
Sparing Your Friends

What you put into your body can affect you in myriad ways, so the dietary decisions you make should be the best possible for your physical and emotional health. It is widely accepted that eating well can help you be more alert and more active, allowing you to accomplish your many goals throughout the year. But many people are under the mistaken impression that eating fruits, vegetables, and grains is the only way to stay healthy; the truth is, there are many foods that are just as good for you (and a lot better for all those innocent members of the plant kingdom!). So please, make meat, poultry, fish, and dairy the centerpieces of your diet, if not your entire diet. Spare your produce pals by never succumbing to the temptation of vegetarianism.

Suddenly, the fridge
didn't seem like such a
bad place after all.

133

SOME VEGETABLES MAY NOT BE GOOD FOR YOU IN THE END

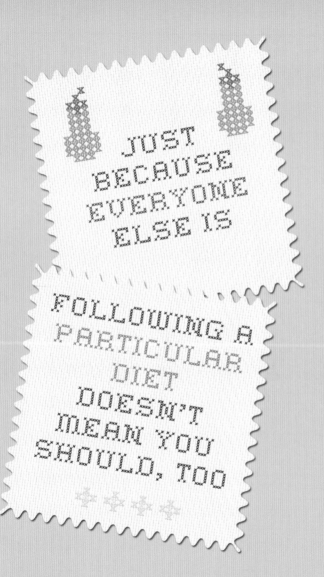

JUST
BECAUSE
EVERYONE
ELSE IS

FOLLOWING A
PARTICULAR
DIET
DOESN'T
MEAN YOU
SHOULD, TOO

The sweet potatoes were led to the chopping board, like yams to the slaughter.

OUR FATES
ARE WRITTEN IN
THE STARS AND
ELSEWHERE

TRY TO BE
RESPECTFUL
OF OTHERS'
EATING HABITS
OR YOU JUST MAY
OFFEND THEM

A

HUNGRY

MAN

IS AN

ANGRY

MAN

Eddie's cow disguise hadn't fooled the vegetarian for one minute.